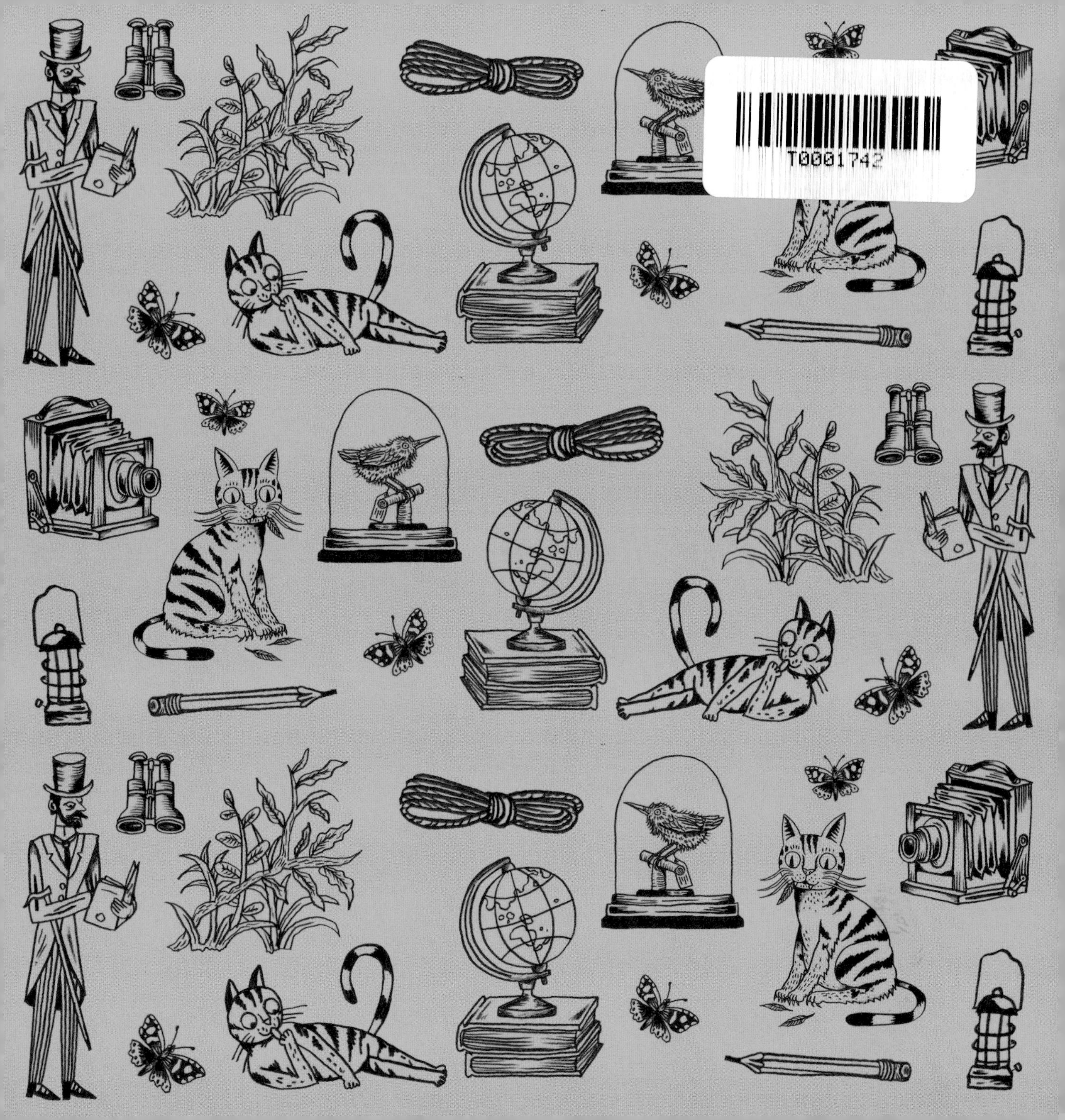

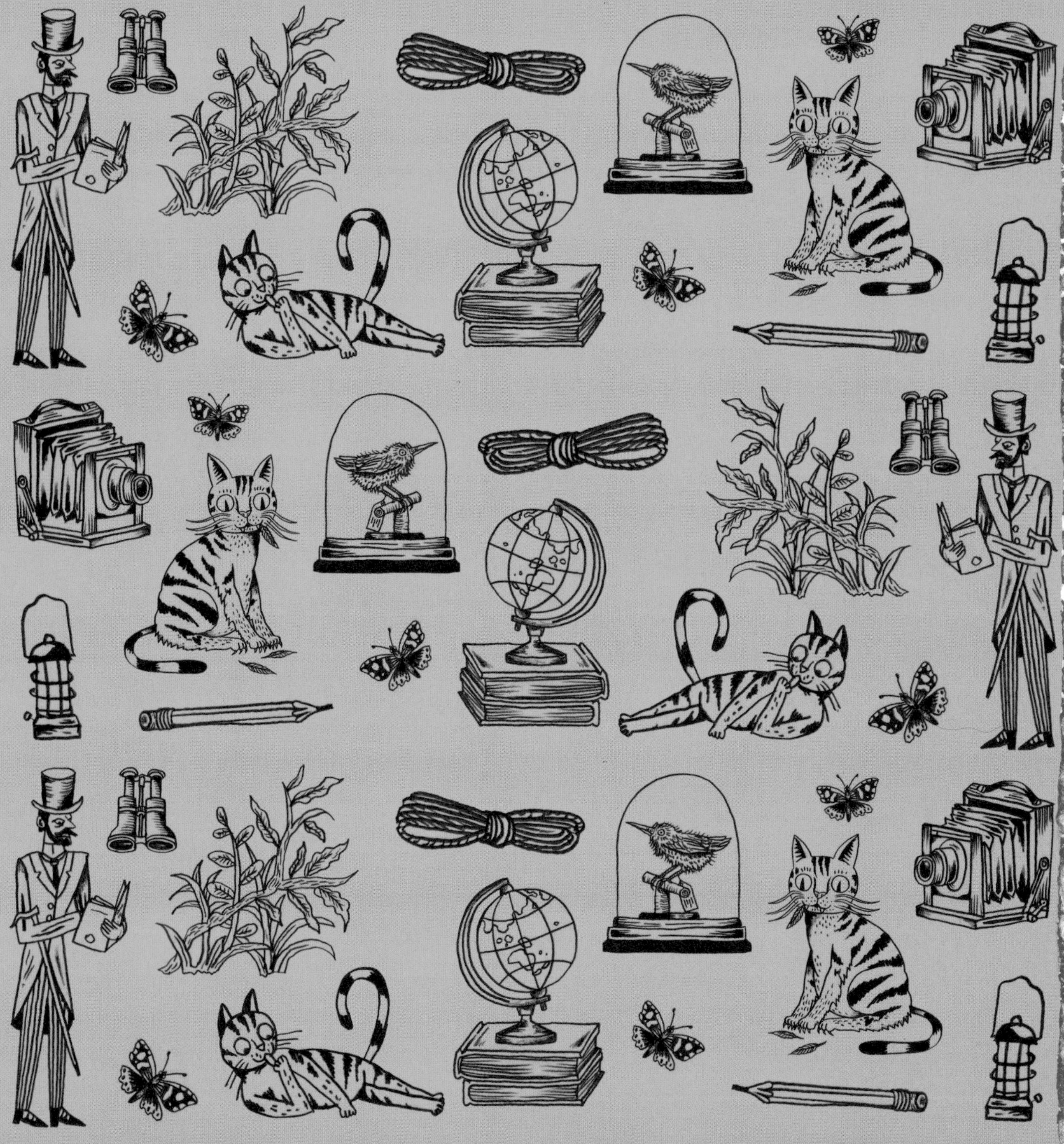

TIBBLES the CAT

Michal Šanda · David Dolenský

© Albatros Media Group, 2023
Originally published by MEANDER, Prague, 2021
5. května 1746/22, Prague 4, Czech Republic
Author: Michal Šanda
Illustrator: David Dolenský
Translator: Mark Worthington
Editor: Scott Alexander Jones

Printed in China by Leo Paper Group.

albatros_books_   Albatros Books
BooksAlbatros   Albatros Media US

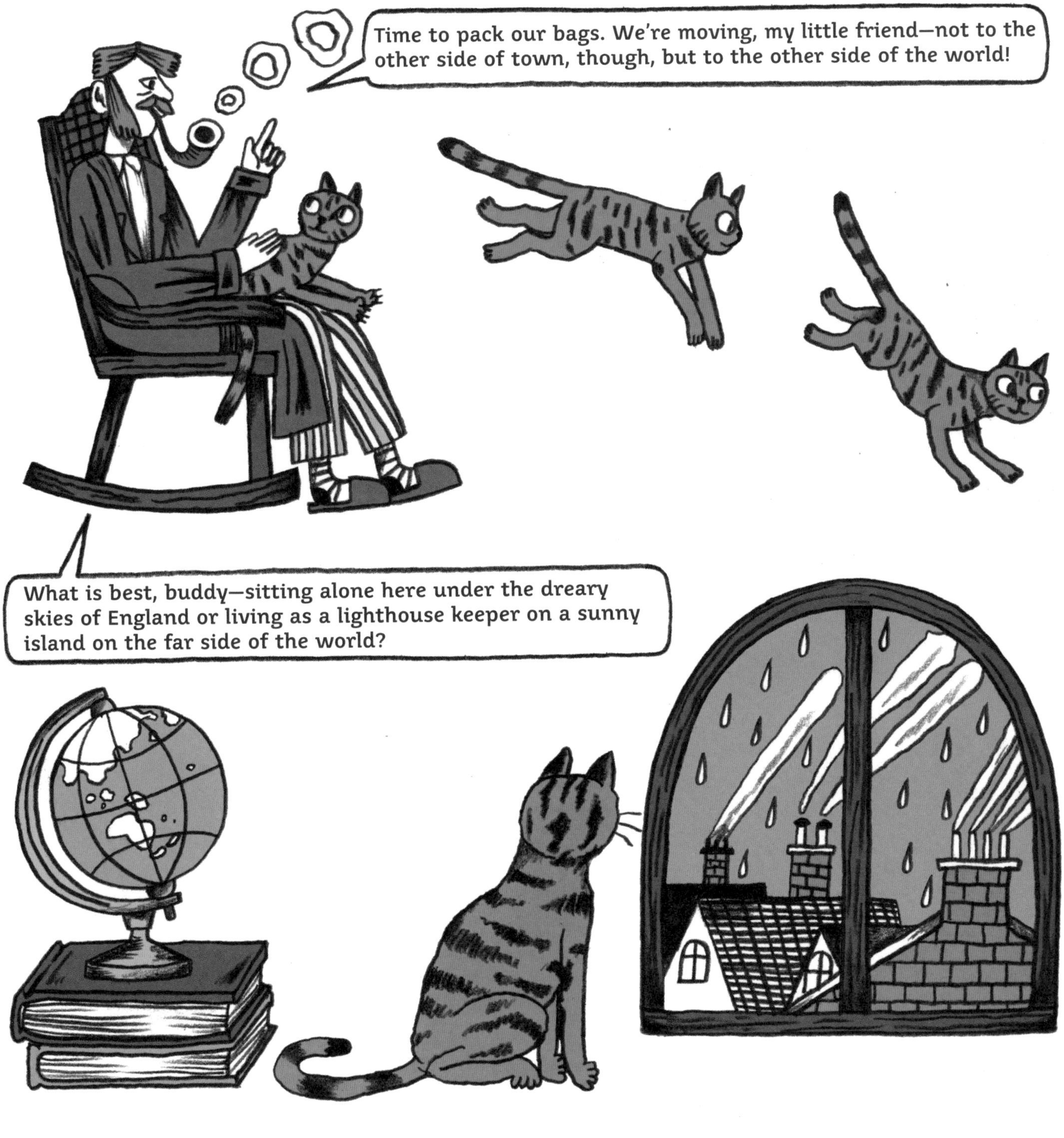
Time to pack our bags. We're moving, my little friend—not to the other side of town, though, but to the other side of the world!
What is best, buddy—sitting alone here under the dreary skies of England or living as a lighthouse keeper on a sunny island on the far side of the world?

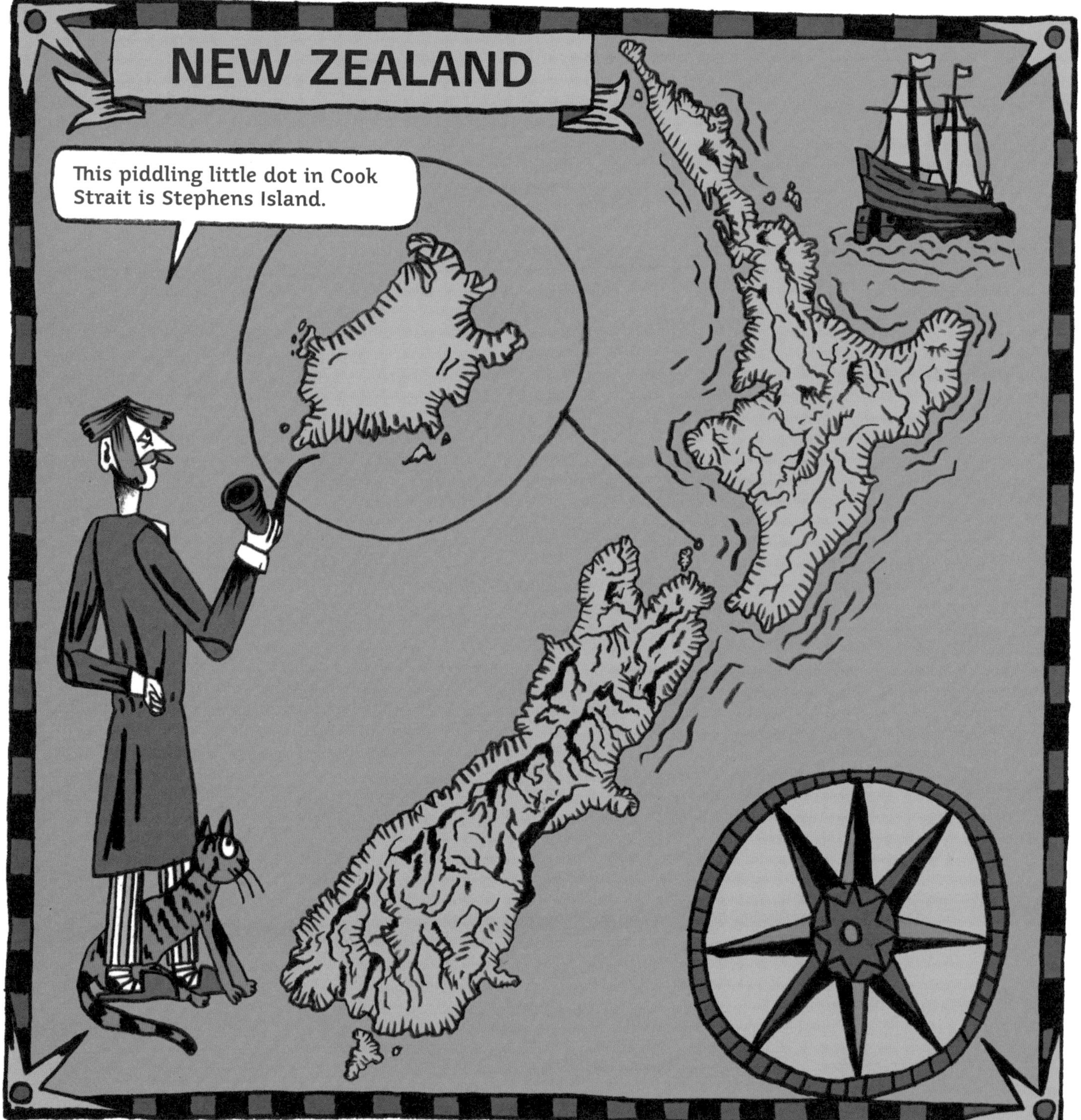
NEW ZEALAND
This piddling little dot in Cook Strait is Stephens Island.

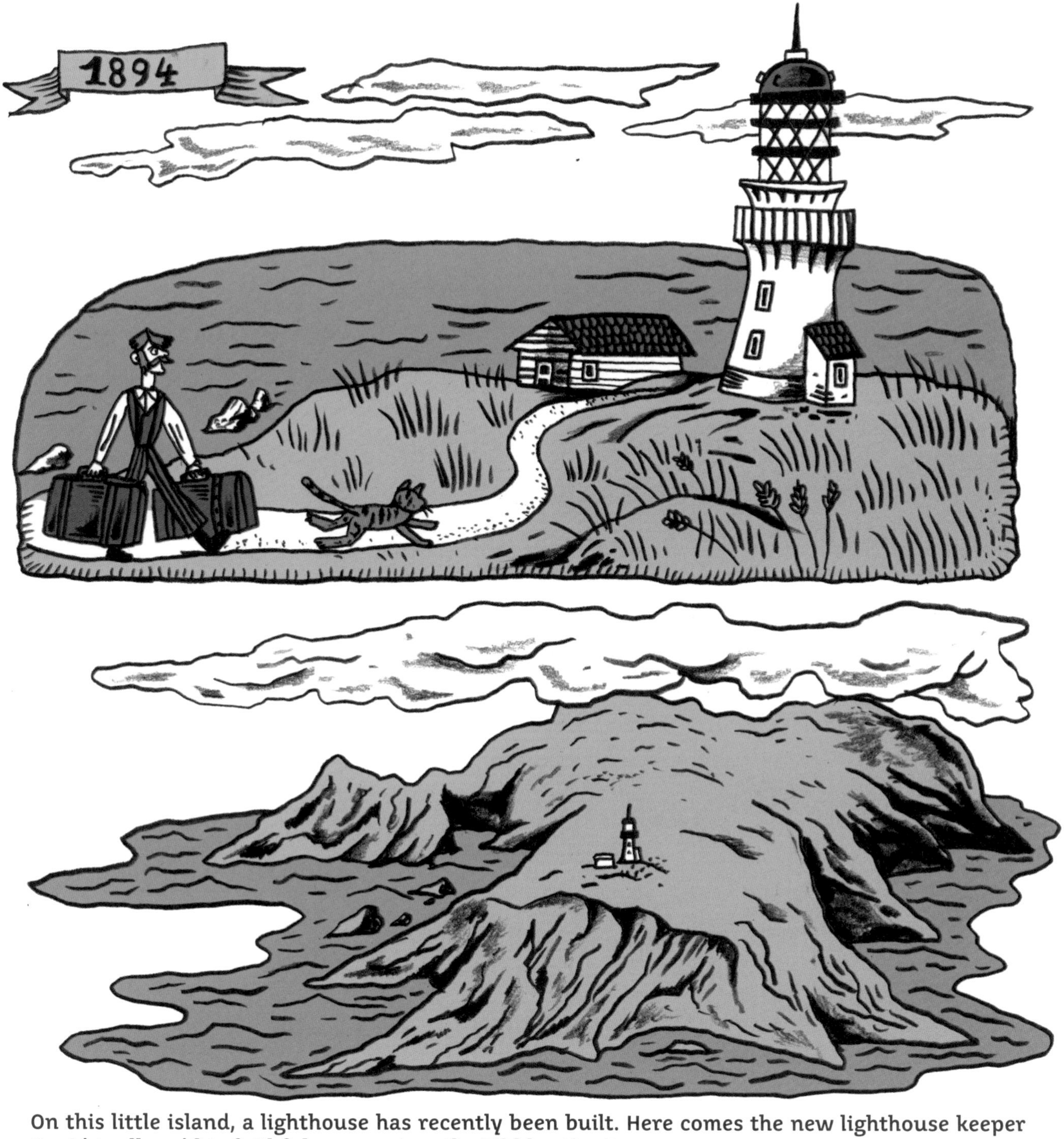
1894

On this little island, a lighthouse has recently been built. Here comes the new lighthouse keeper David Lyall and his faithful companion, the Tibbles the Cat.

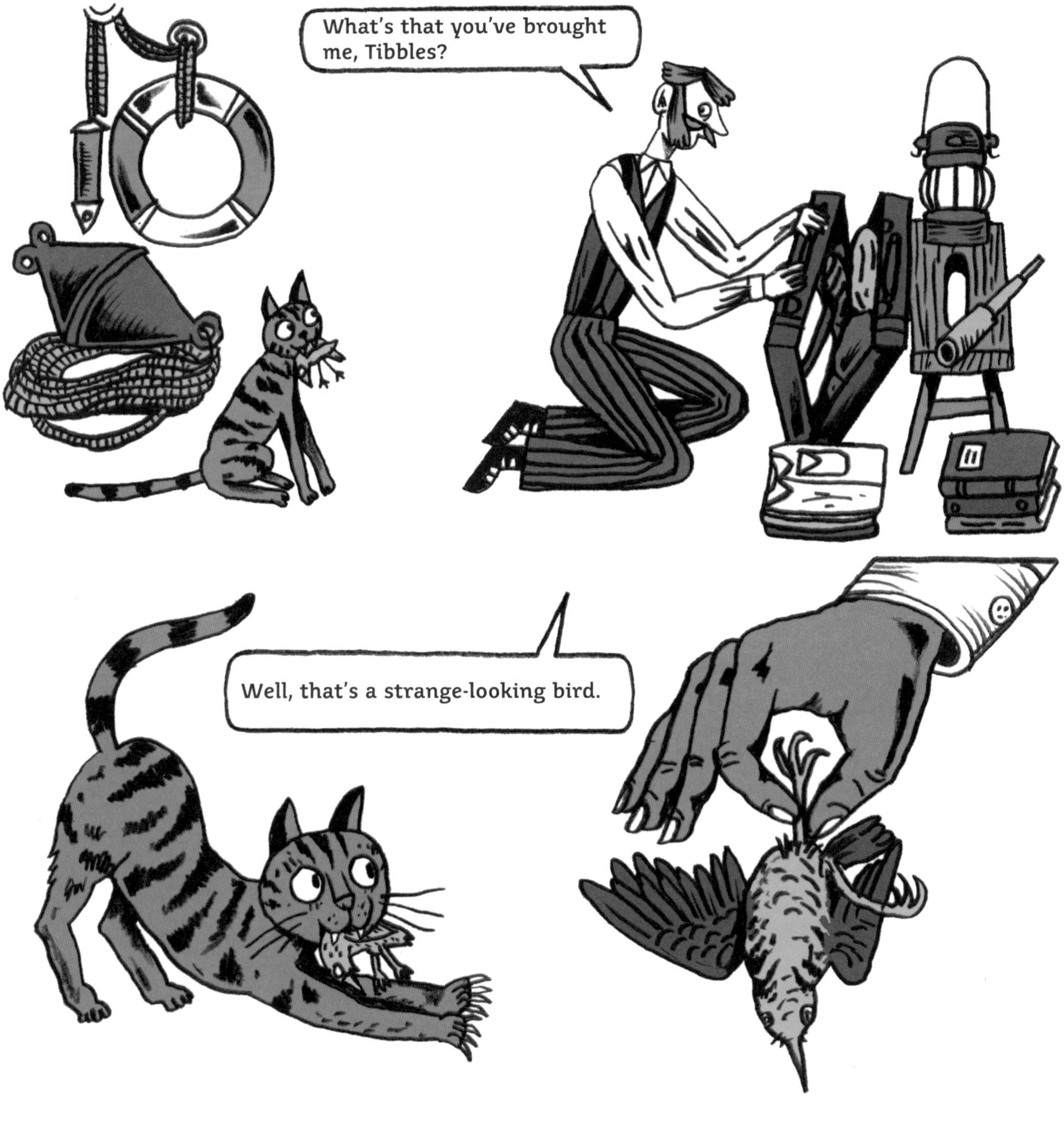
What's that you've brought me, Tibbles?
Well, that's a strange-looking bird.

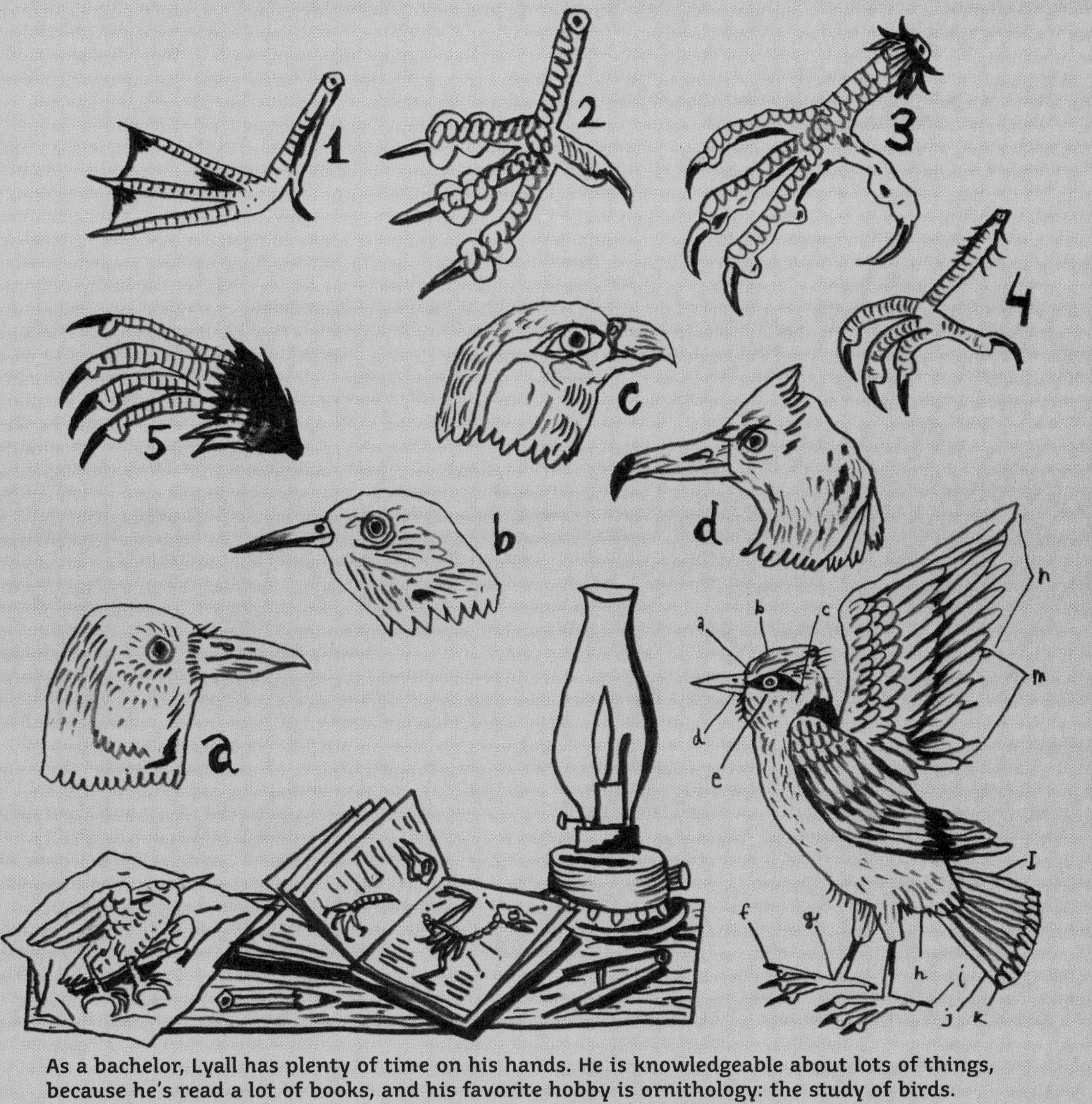
1
2
3
4
5
a
b
c
d
a
b
c
d
e
f
g
h
i
j
k
I
m
n

As a bachelor, Lyall has plenty of time on his hands. He is knowledgeable about lots of things, because he's read a lot of books, and his favorite hobby is ornithology: the study of birds. But never before has he seen such a strange bird in any of his books.

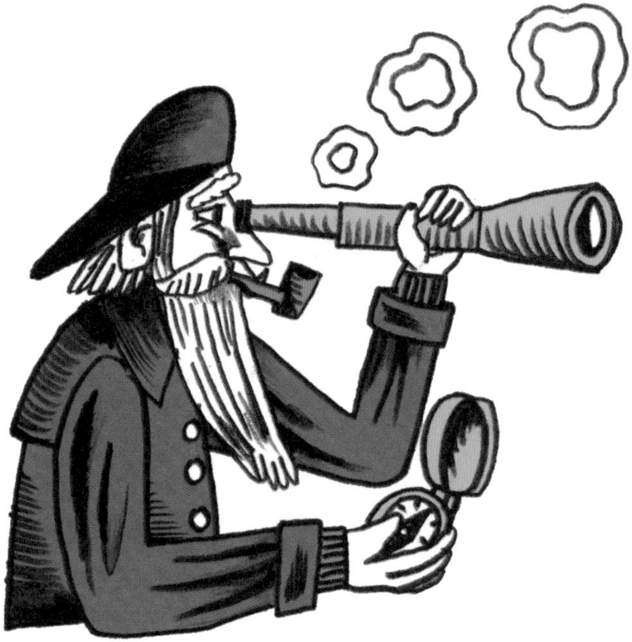

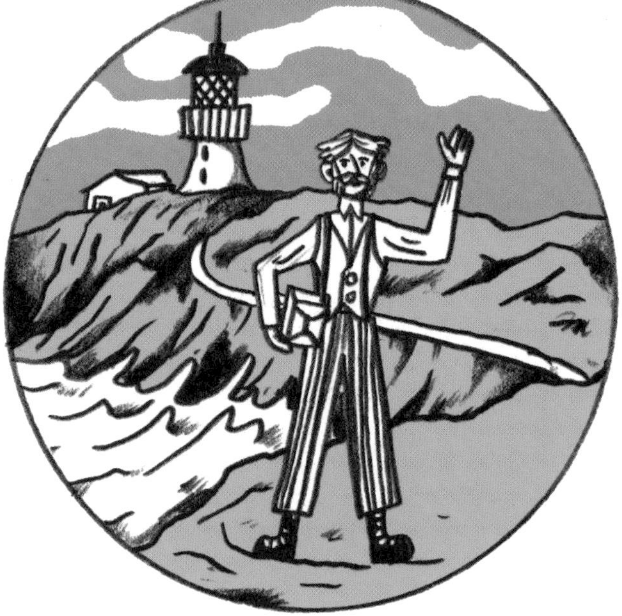

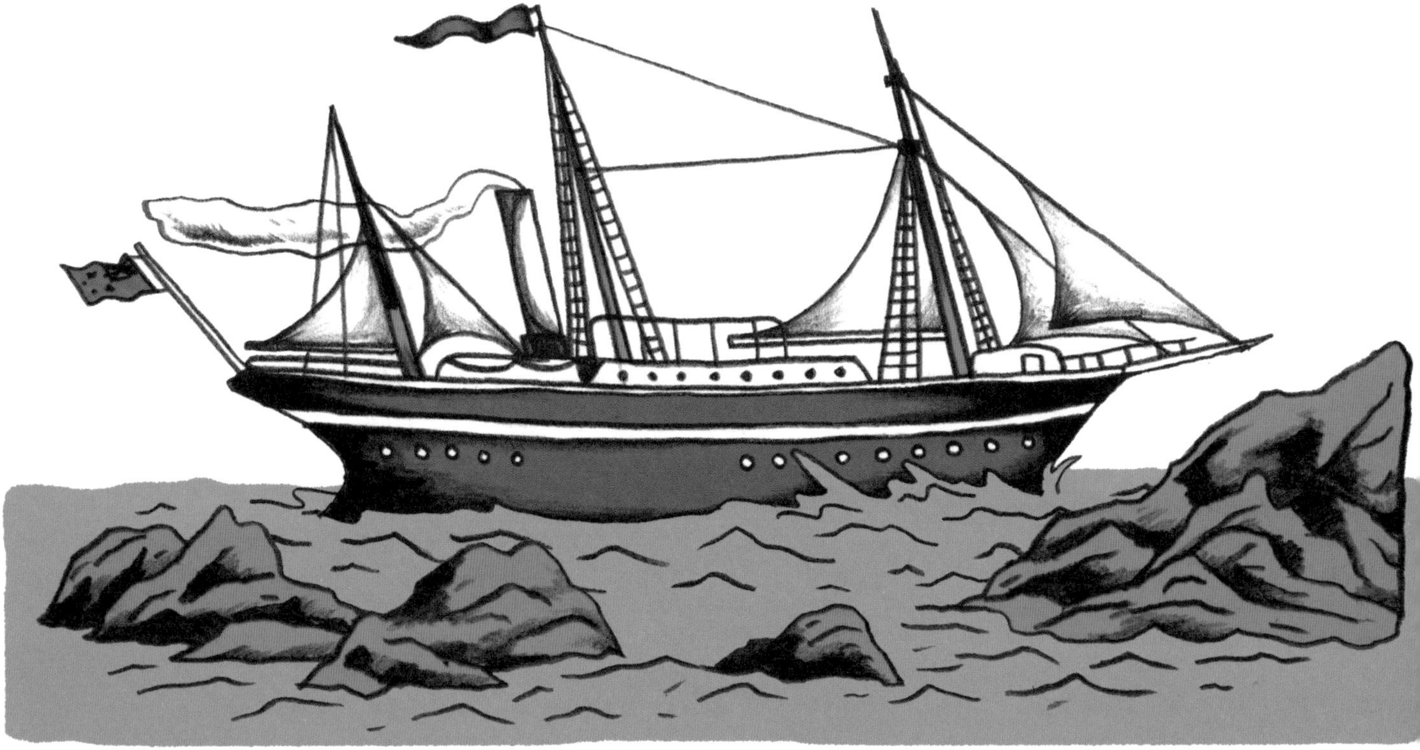

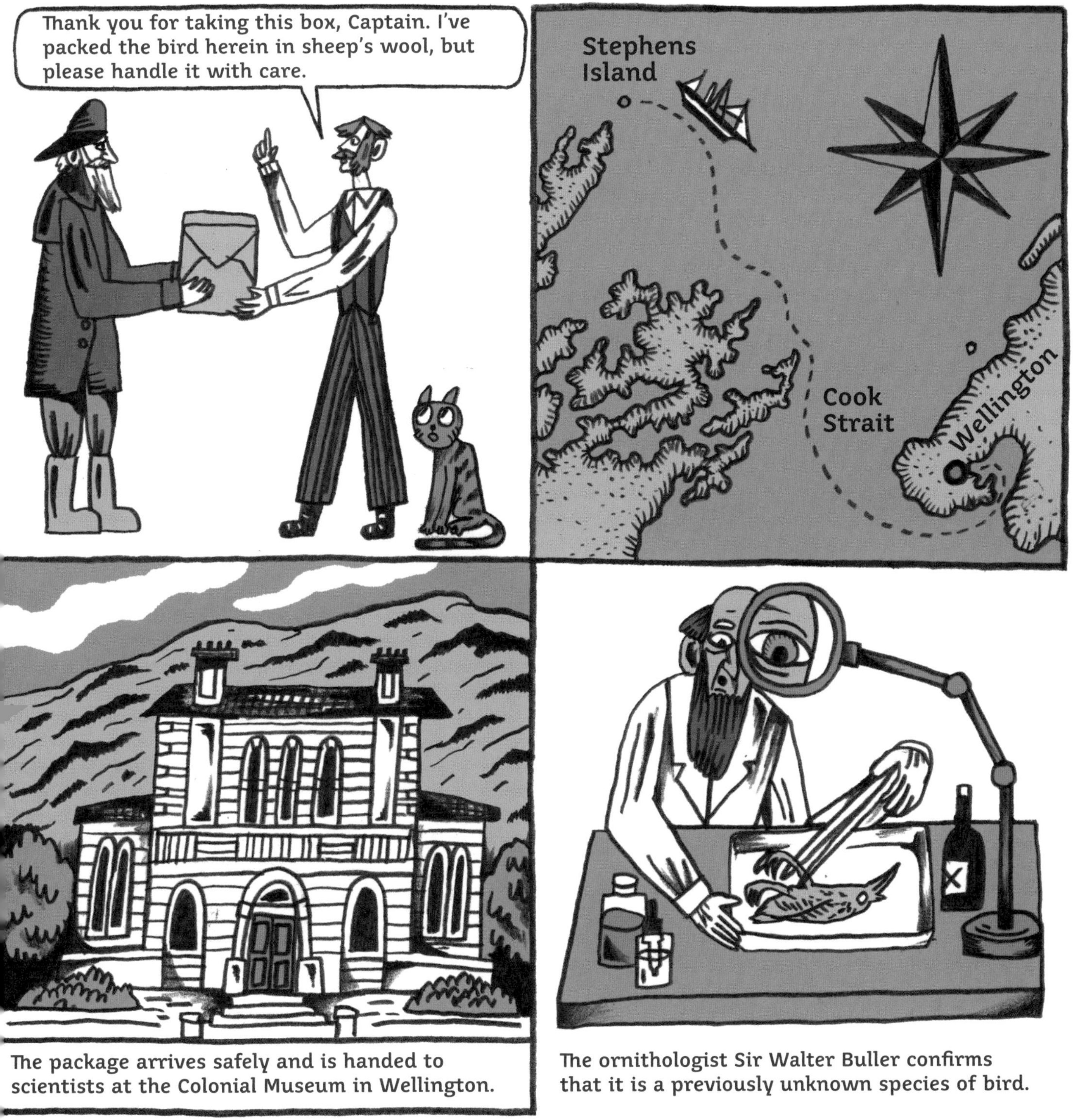
Thank you for taking this box, Captain. I've packed the bird herein in sheep's wool, but please handle it with care.
Stephens Island
Cook Strait
Wellington
The package arrives safely and is handed to scientists at the Colonial Museum in Wellington.
The ornithologist Sir Walter Buller confirms that it is a previously unknown species of bird.

In London, the illustrator John Gerrard Keulemans makes a lithographic plate of the specimen that has been sent to him.

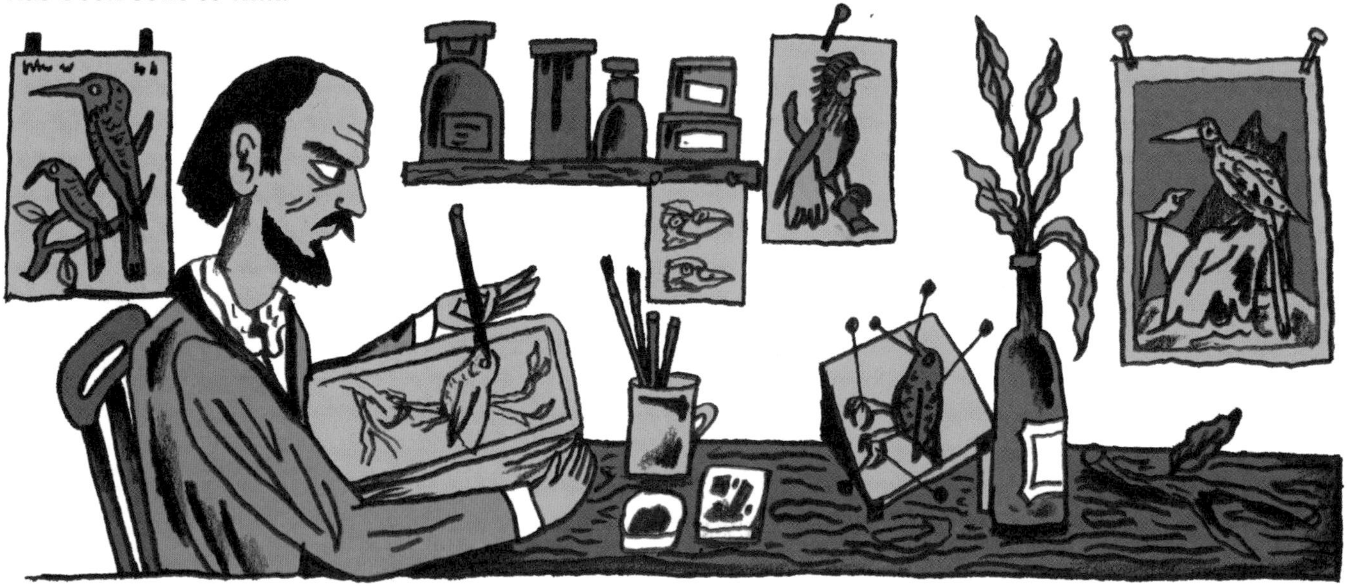

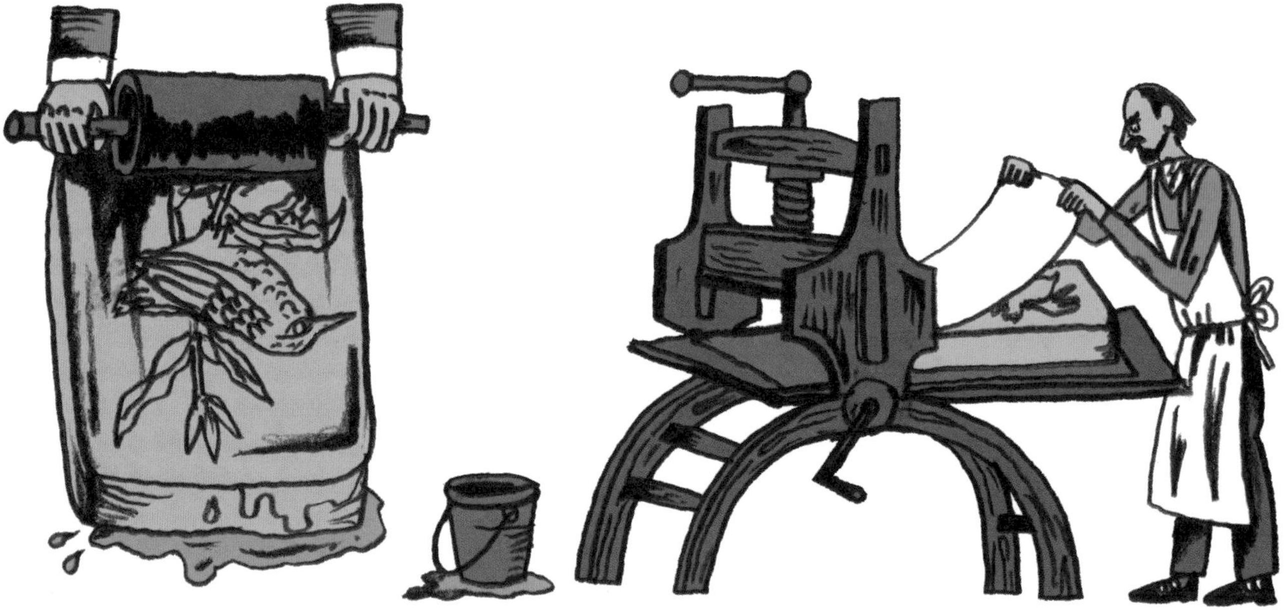

He rolls the paint onto a limestone block. The paint only adheres to those parts that have been drawn in grease pencil. With this printmaking technique, he prints the drawing on a lithographic press in his workshop.

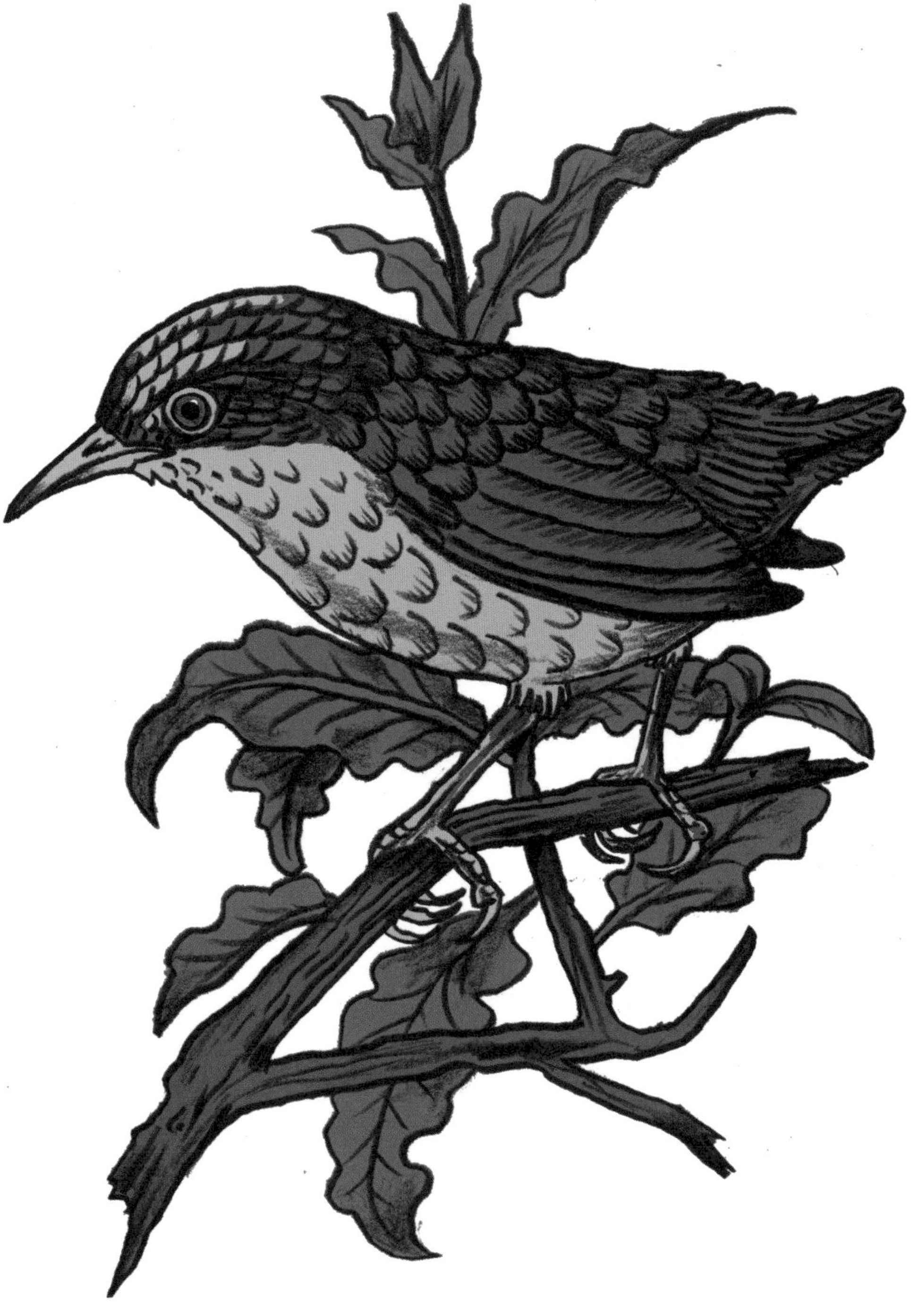

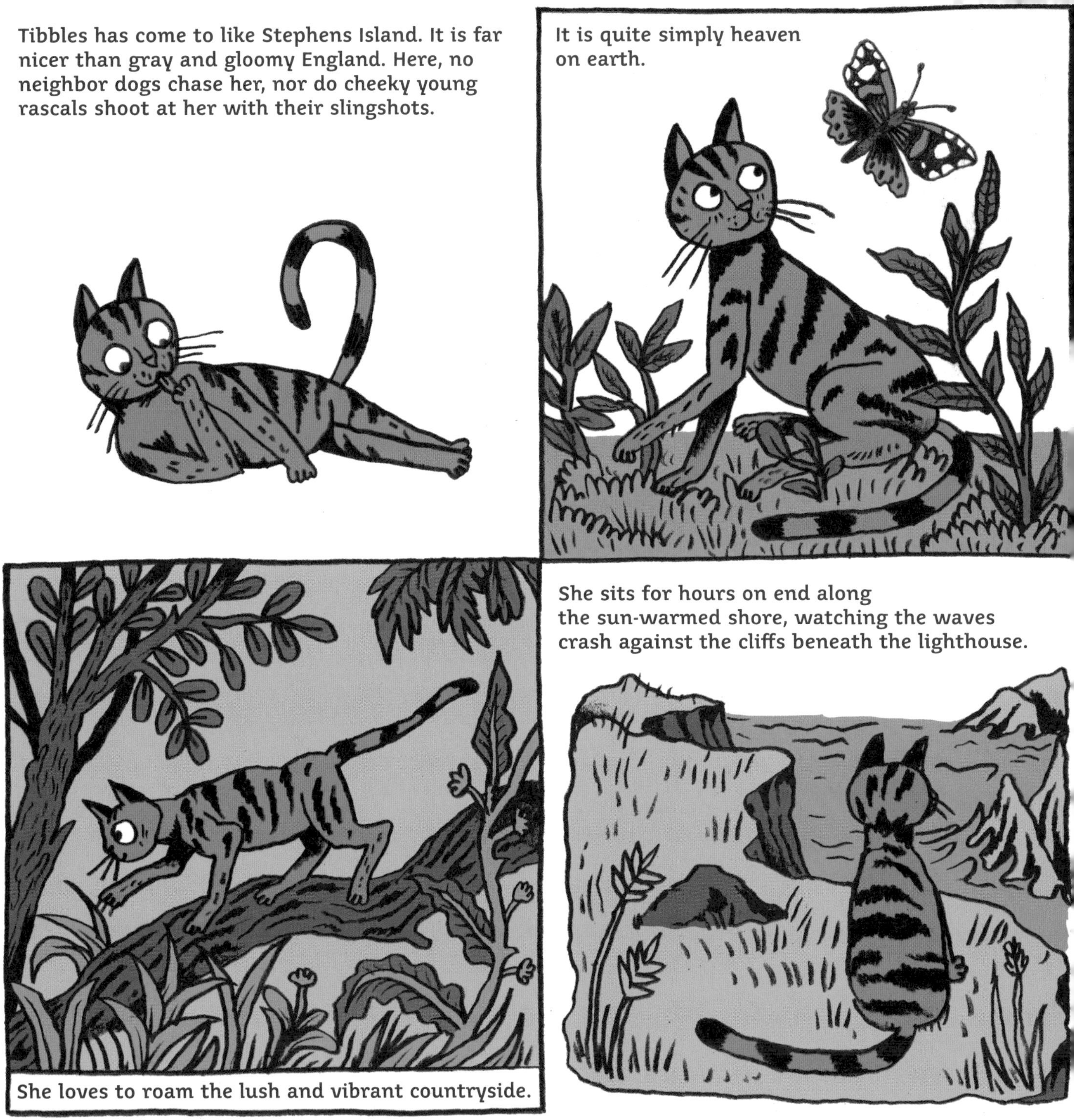
Tibbles has come to like Stephens Island. It is far nicer than gray and gloomy England. Here, no neighbor dogs chase her, nor do cheeky young rascals shoot at her with their slingshots.
It is quite simply heaven on earth.
She loves to roam the lush and vibrant countryside.
She sits for hours on end along the sun-warmed shore, watching the waves crash against the cliffs beneath the lighthouse.

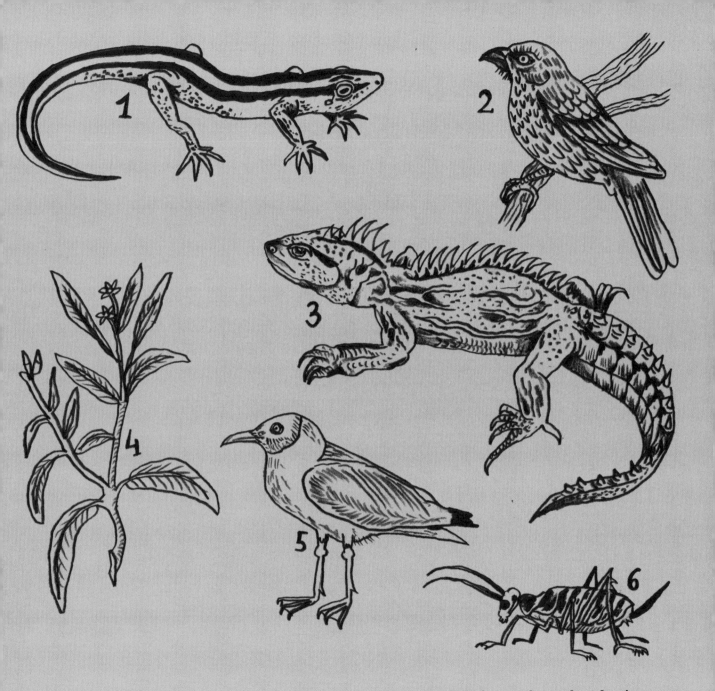

Tibbles has also become well acquainted with the diverse plants and animals on the island:
1. Stephens Island geko 2. Stephens Island piopio 3. Tuatara 4. Cheesewood plant
5. Red-billed gull 6. Wētā

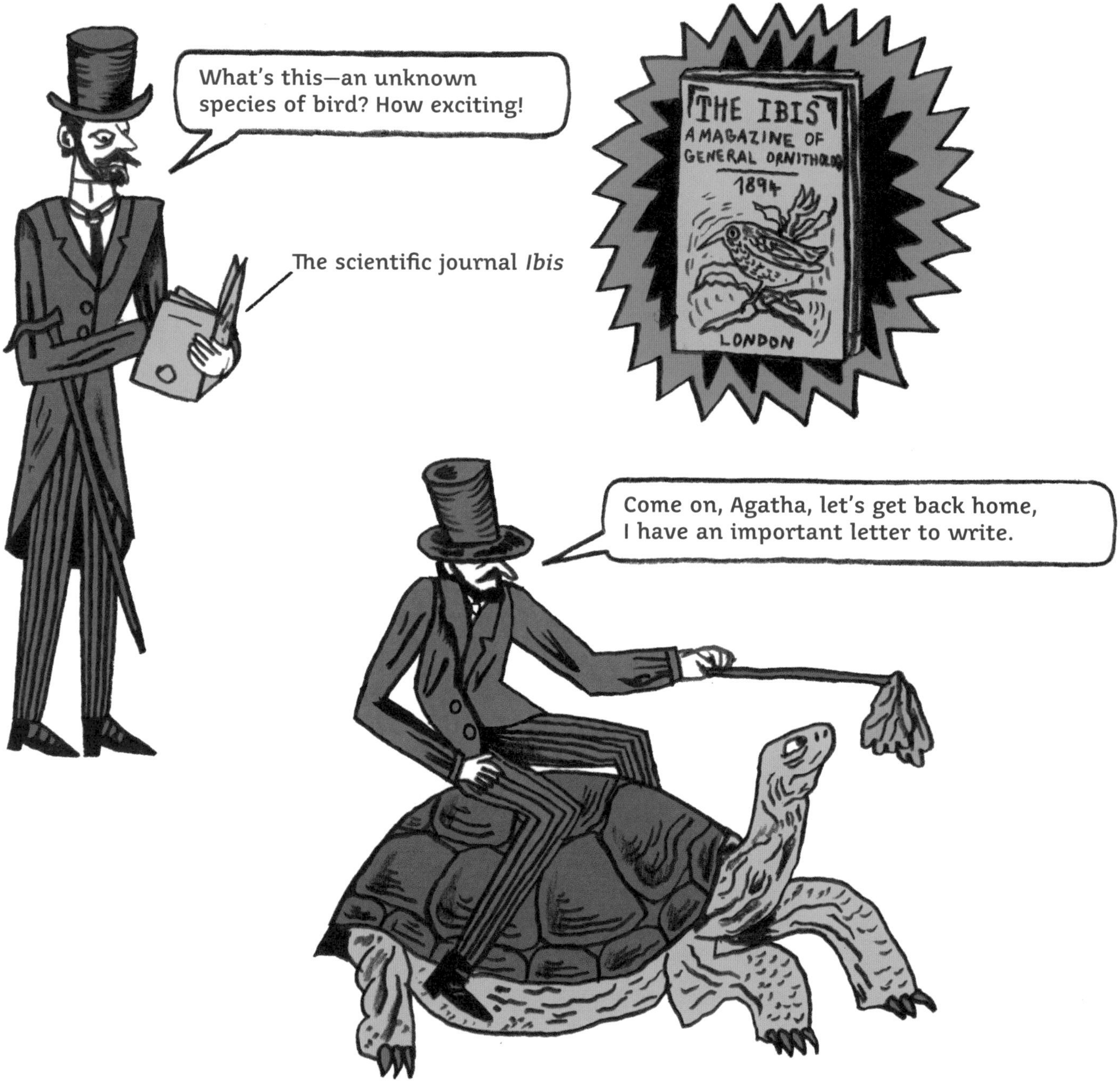
What's this—an unknown species of bird? How exciting!
The scientific journal *Ibis*
THE IBIS
A MAGAZINE OF
1894
LONDON
Come on, Agatha, let's get back home, I have an important letter to write.

Baron Lionel Walter Rothschild comes from a wealthy family of bankers, famous the world over. Even so, he himself has no particular talent for banking. He is well aware that after we die our wealth means nothing—"Unlike a tuxedo," he says, "a shroud has no pockets"—so he has donated most of his money to research to the natural sciences.

Later, when he grows old and looks back on his life, his zoological collection will be the largest in the world, containing 300,000 birds, 200,000 bird eggs, over 2 million butterflies, 30,000 beetles, and thousands upon thousands of species of mammals, lizards, and fish. Naturally, he had to have this newly discovered bird in his collection.

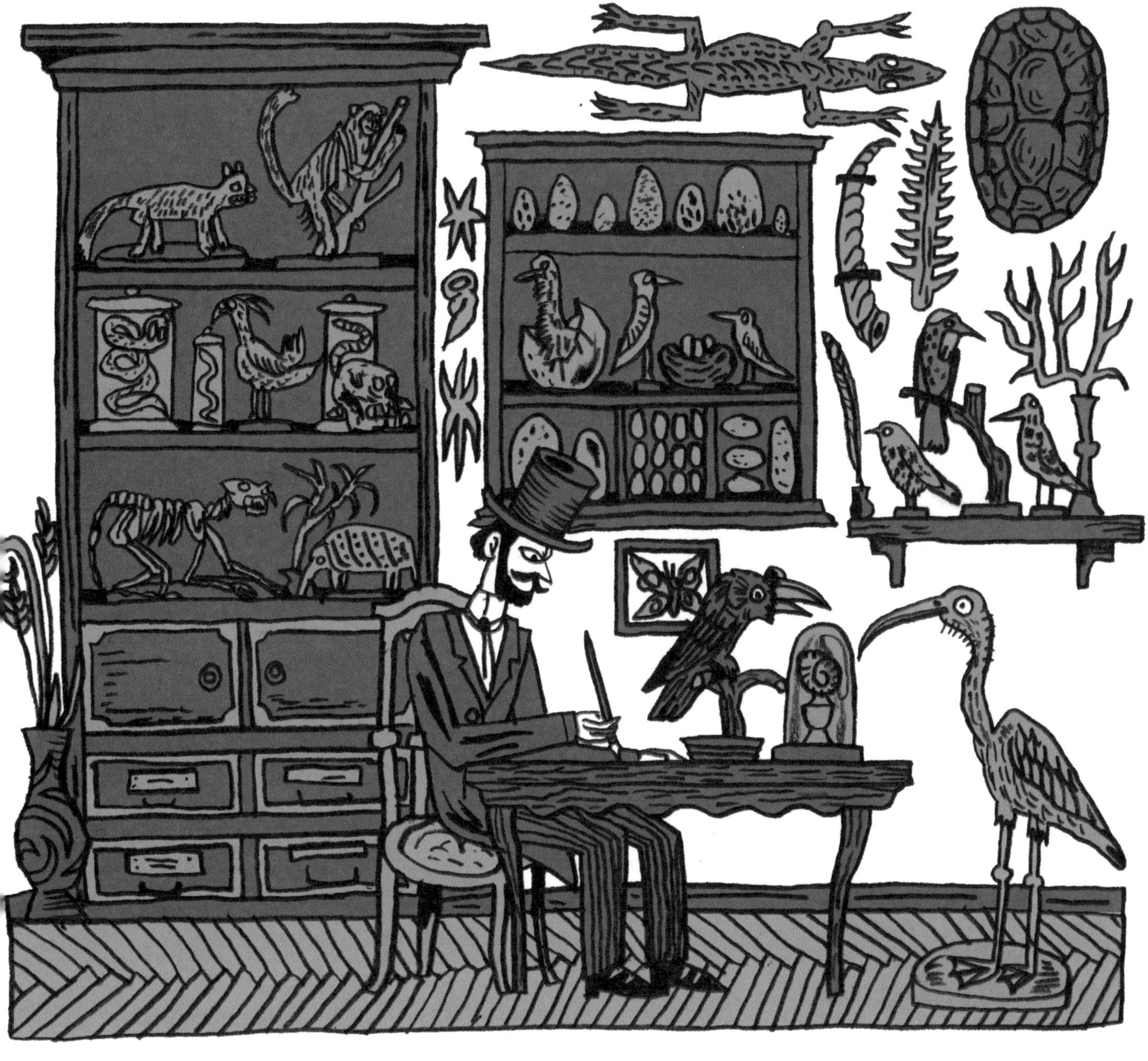

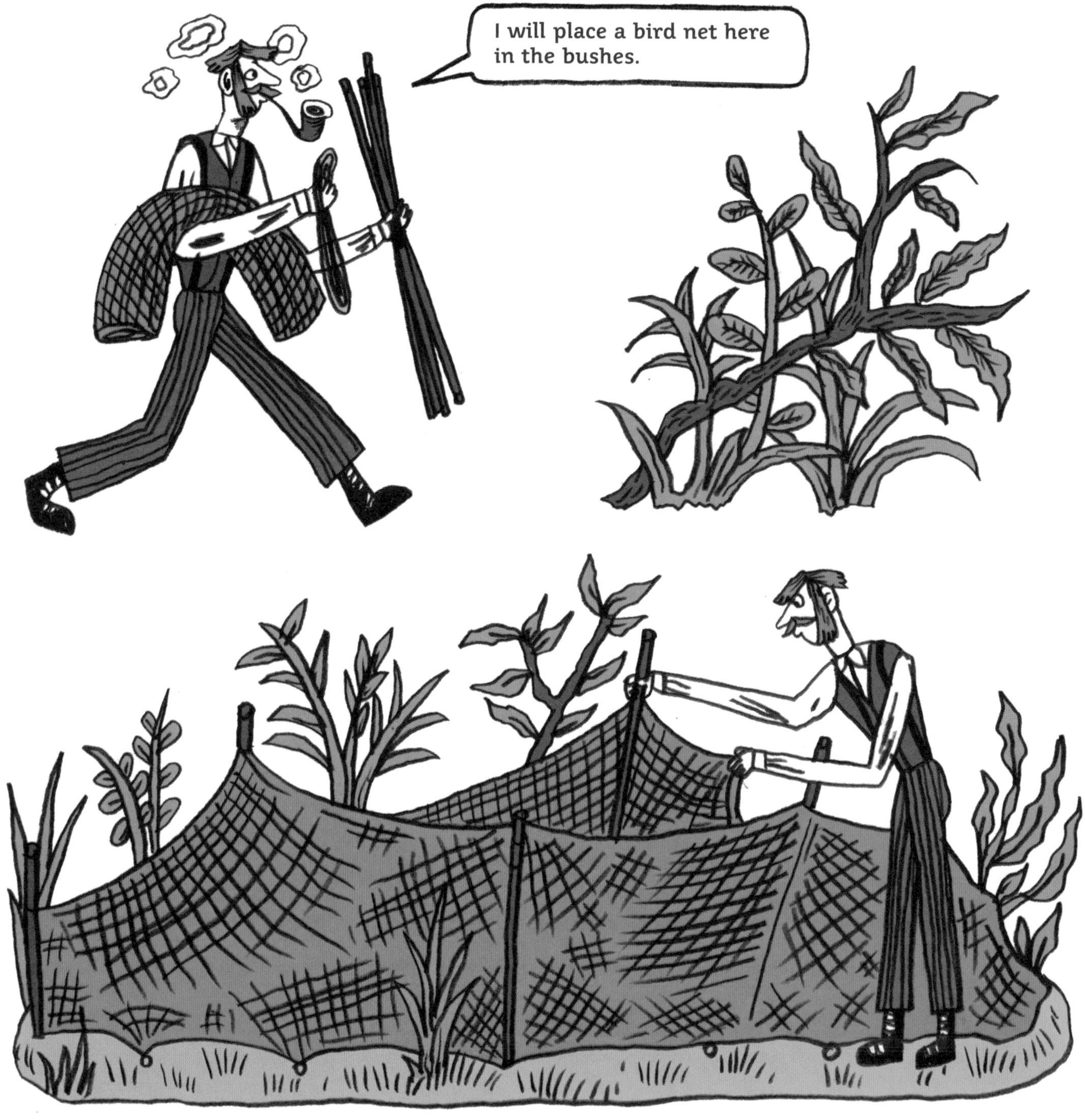
I will place a bird net here in the bushes.

At the request of Baron Rothschild, the nine specimens that Lyall caught arrive in England.

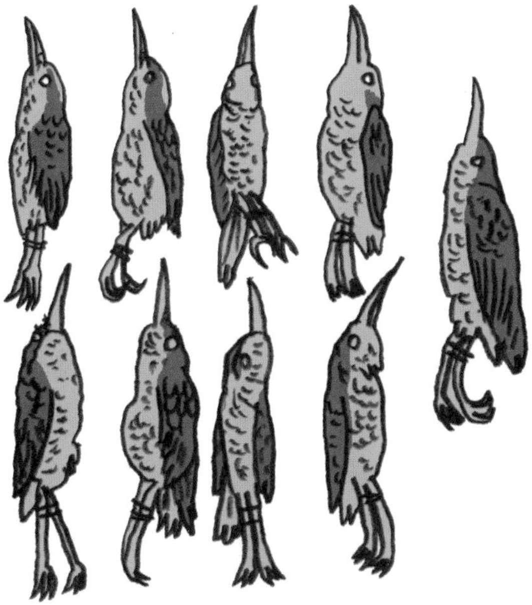

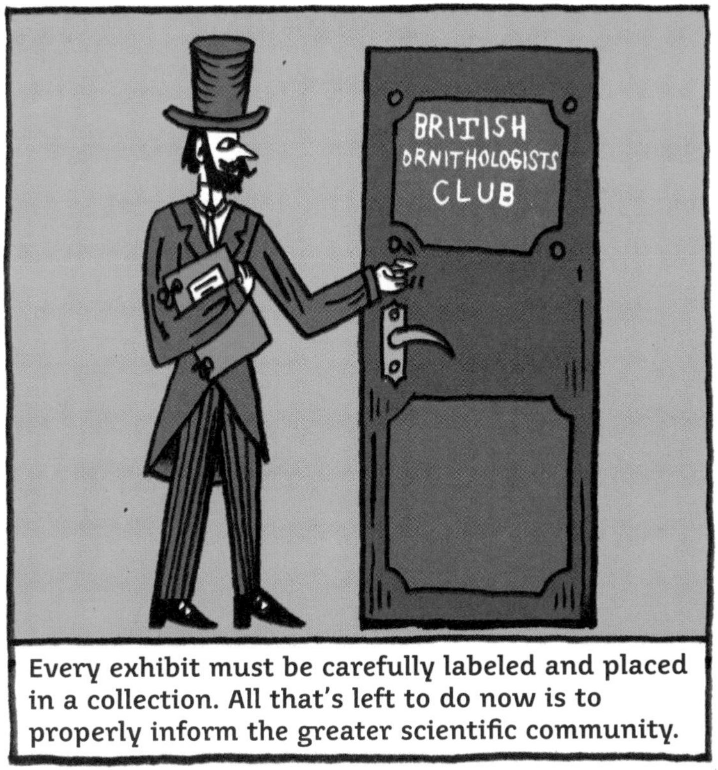
BRITISH
ORNITHOLOGISTS
CLUB
Every exhibit must be carefully labeled and placed in a collection. All that's left to do now is to properly inform the greater scientific community.

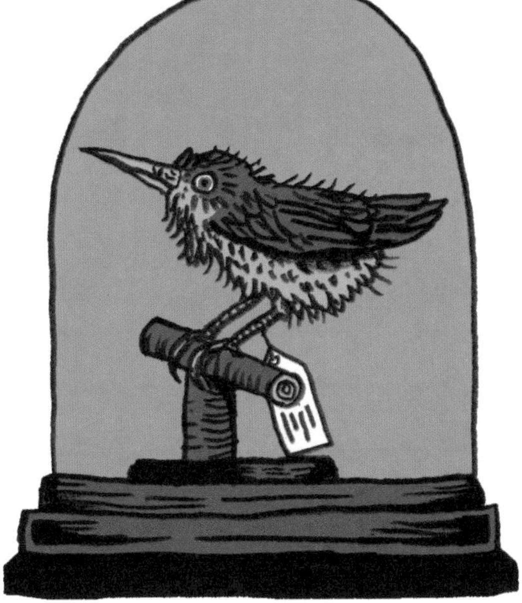

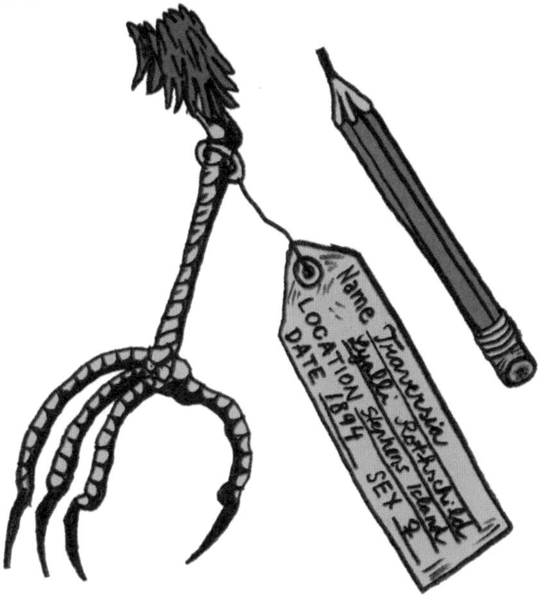
Name Traversia
Lyalli Rothschild
LOCATION Stephens Island
DATE 1894 SEX

The bird is named the Stephens Island wren. And in honor of both Lyall and New Zealand naturalist Henry Travers, who sold some specimens to his friend and colleague Baron Rothschild, Rothschild gives it the Latin name *Traversia lyalli*.

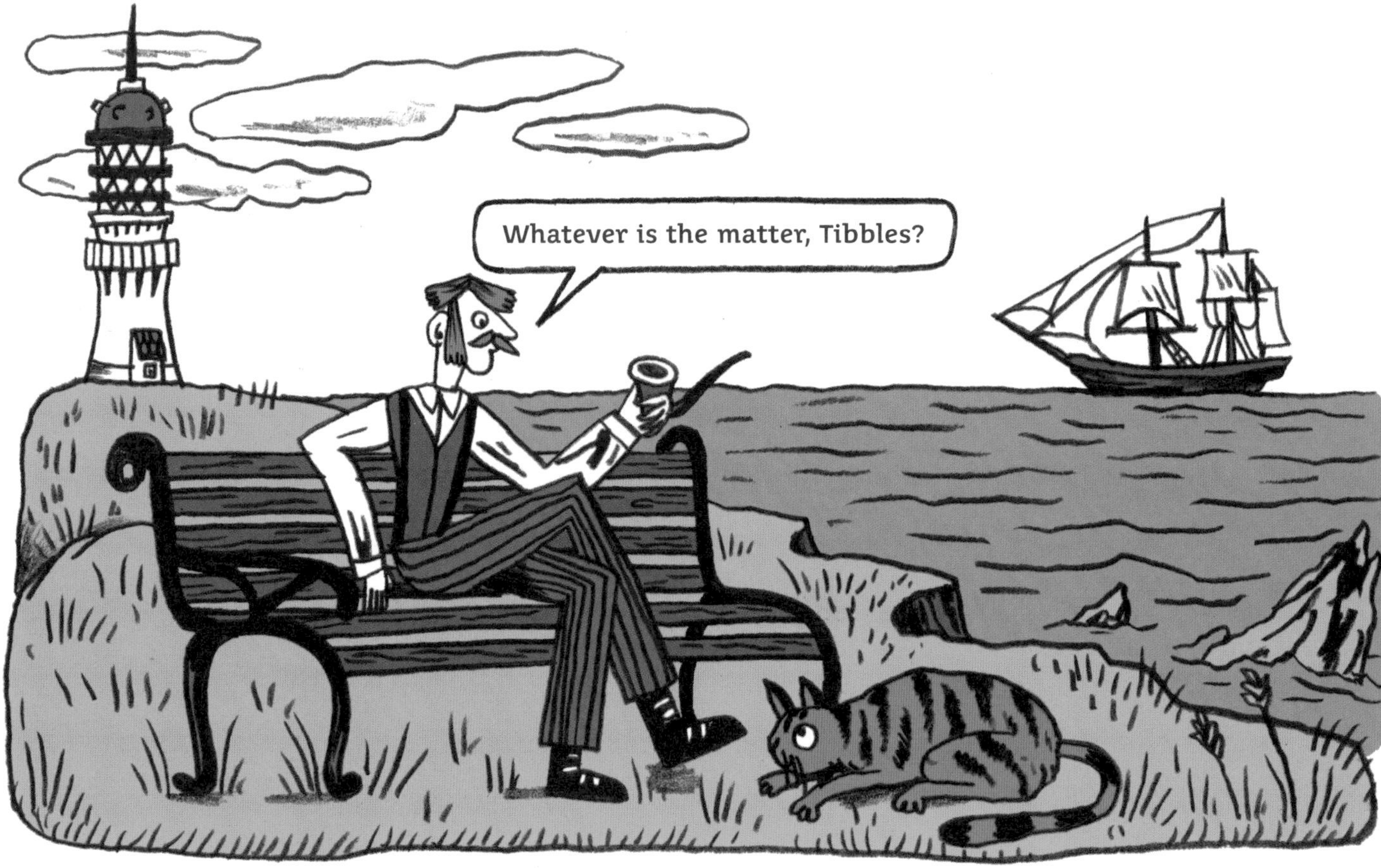
Whatever is the matter, Tibbles?

Having received a great deal of money from Rothschild, Lyall is able to treat his furry little friend to the finest delicacies, which he orders from Sydney in nearby Australia. He serves her salmon fillets in caviar, but curiously, Tibbles won't even touch her food. Even so, she is growing quite fat—so much so that she is like a ball, one that could barely roll. Perhaps she has caught some insidious disease . . .

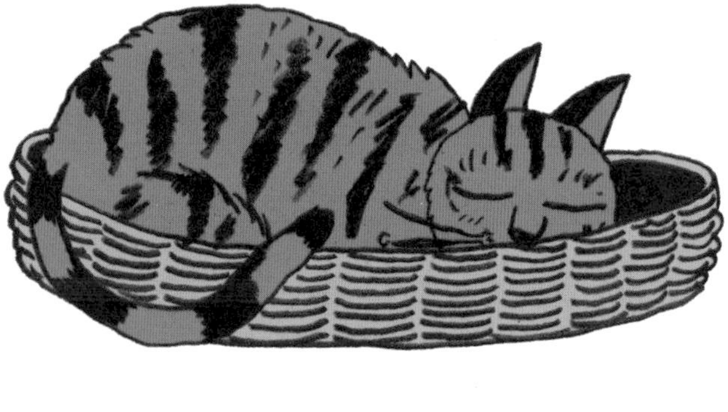

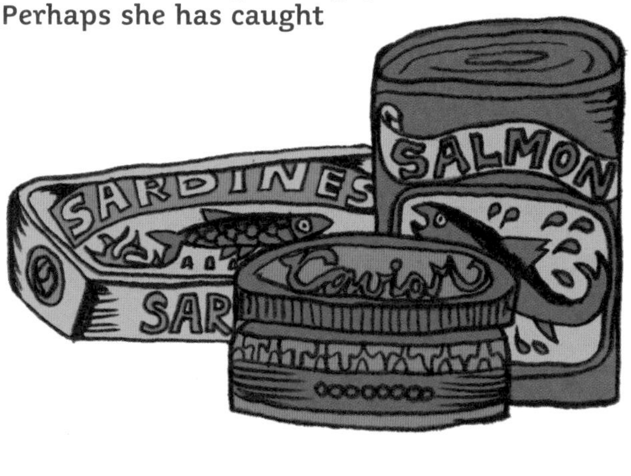
SARDINES
SALMON
Caviar

A delegation from the British Ornithologists' Club arrives on Stephens Island.

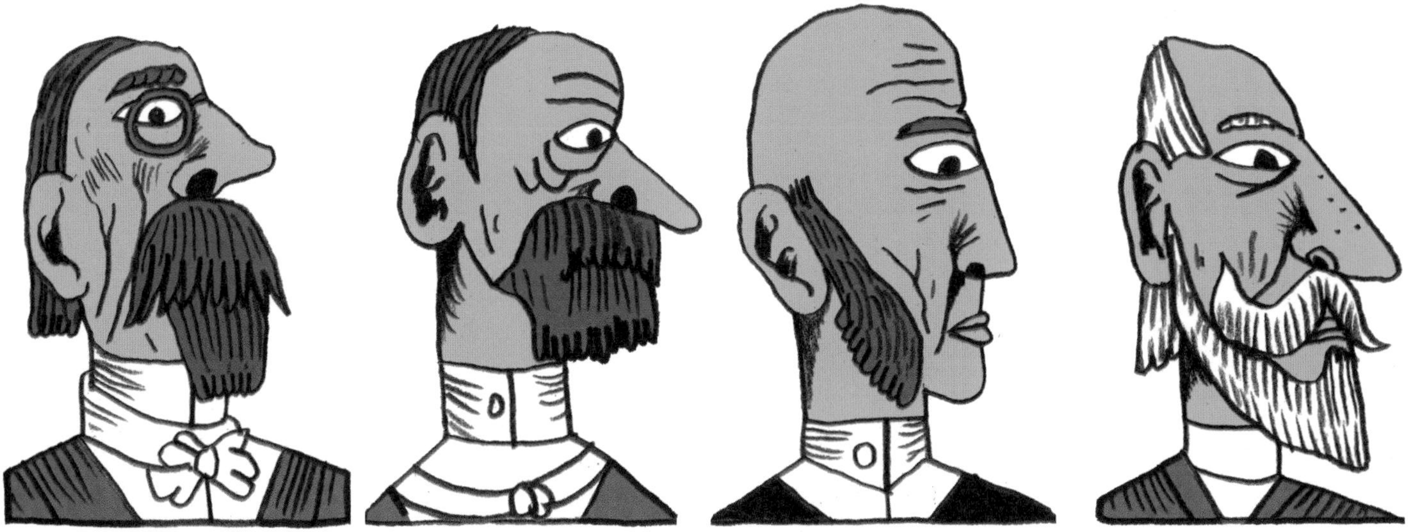

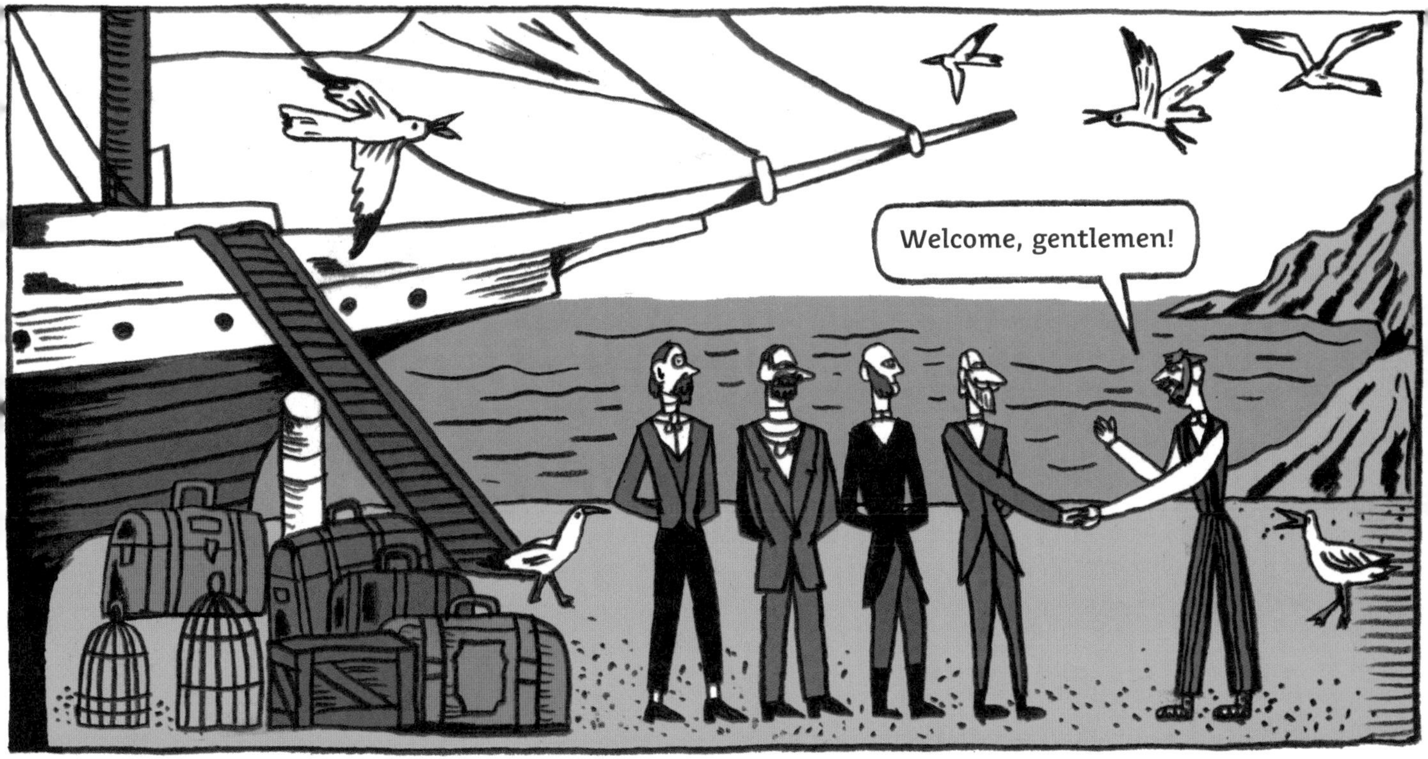
Welcome, gentlemen!

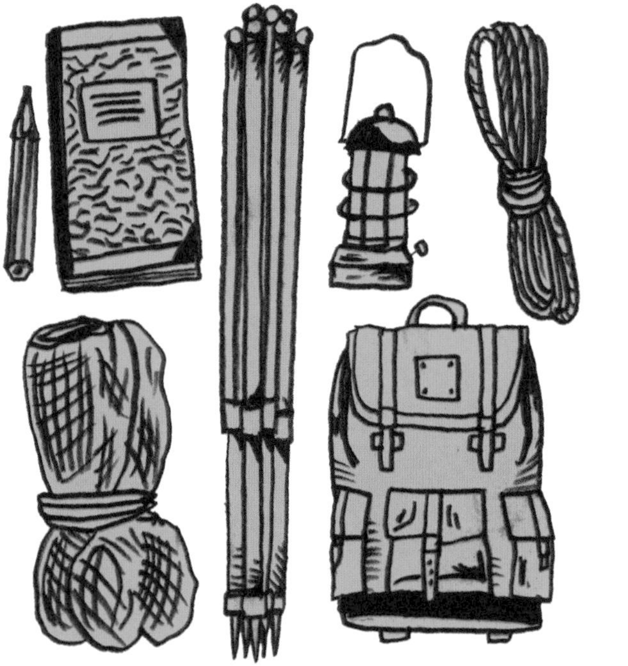

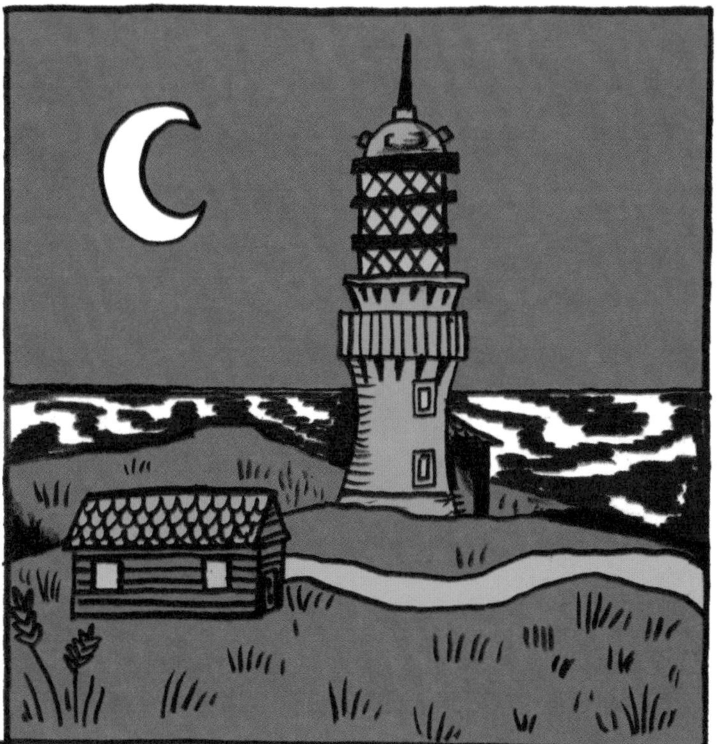

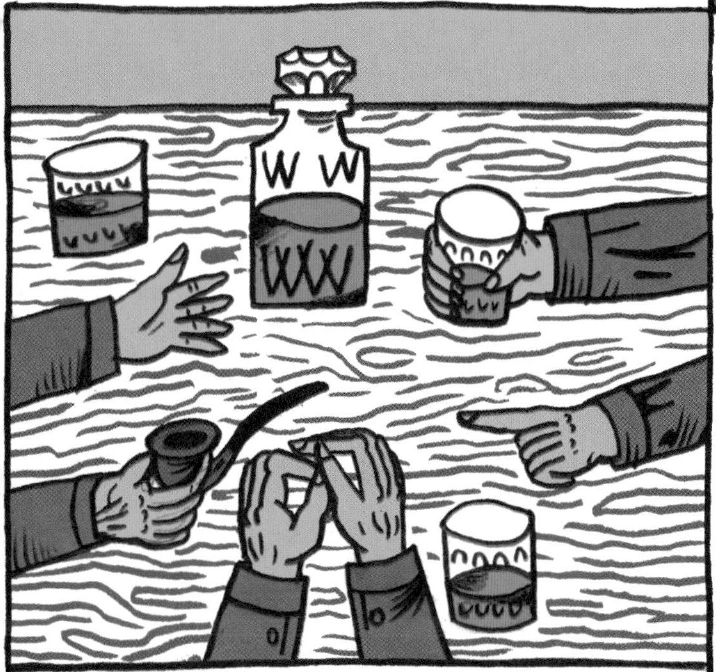

In the evening, they discuss scientific issues with great excitement and make plans for the next day.

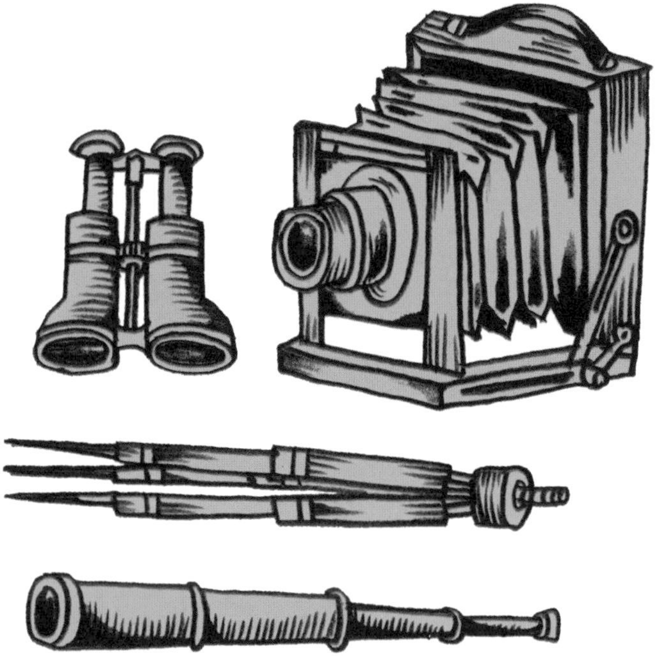

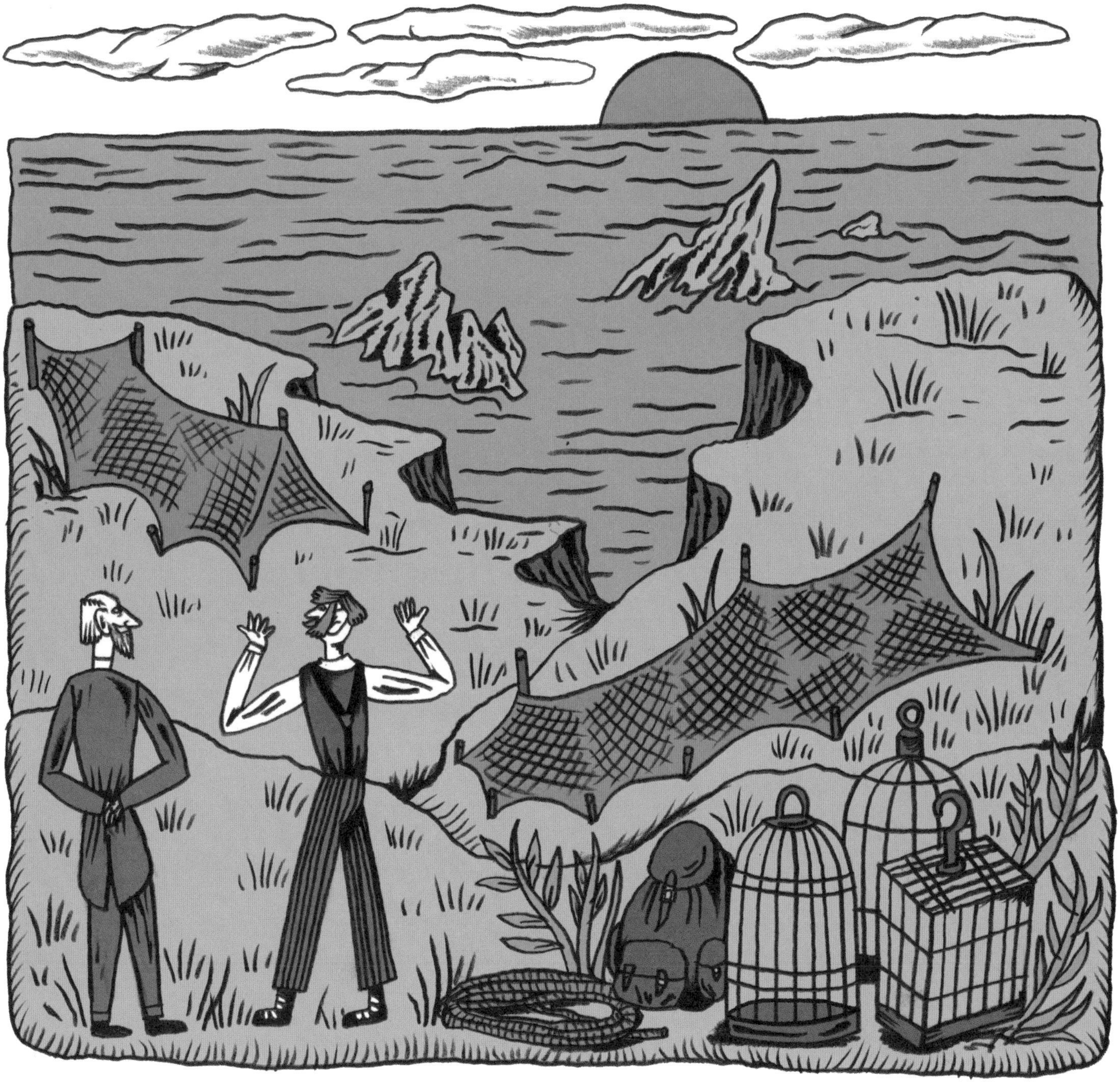

Although the island is teeming with nets, they cannot catch a single Stephens Island wren.

Oh no! That's why Tibbles has grown so fat! In less than a year, she has hunted to extinction the very bird she famously discovered.

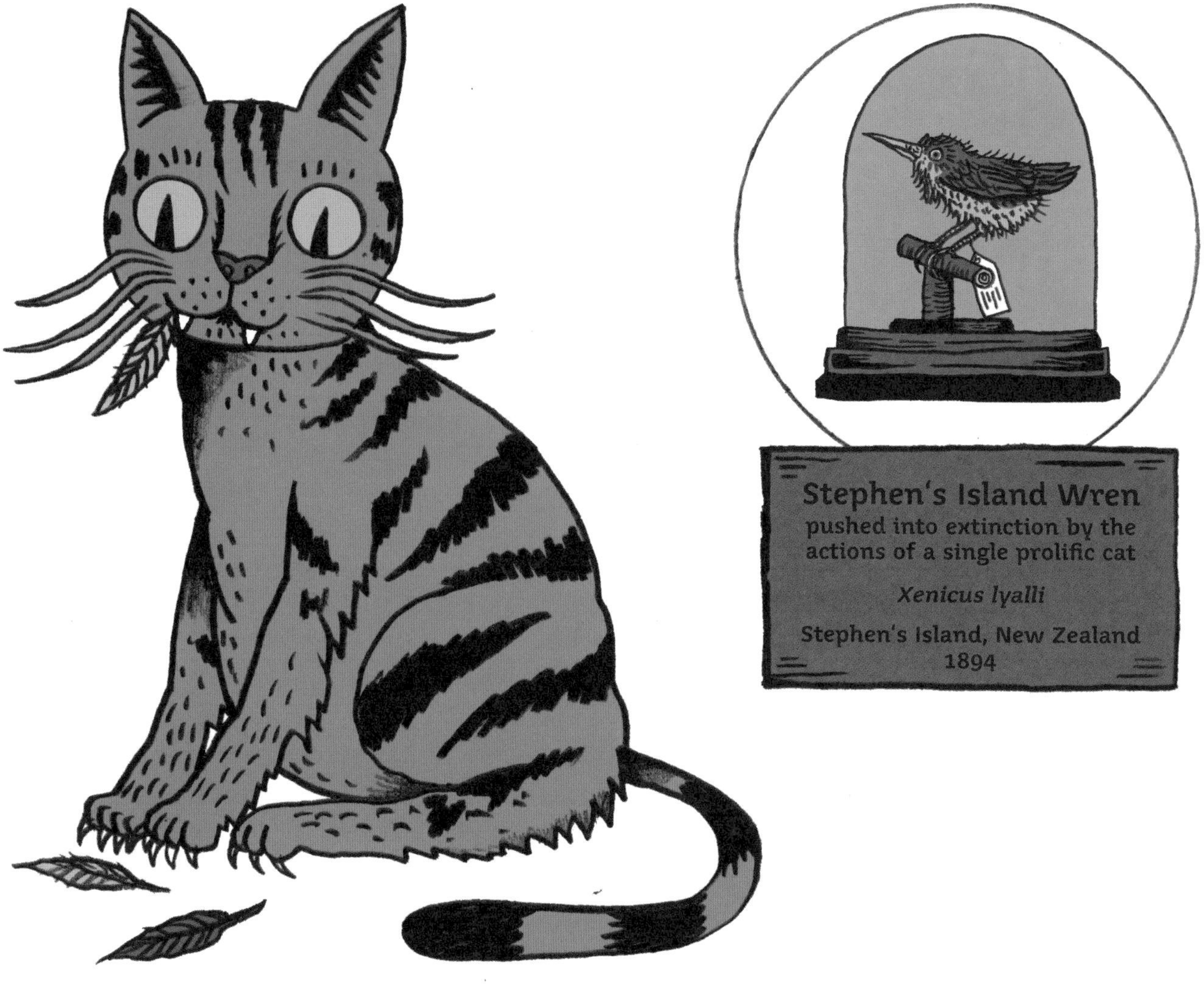
Stephen's Island Wren
pushed into extinction by the actions of a single prolific cat
Xenicus lyalli
Stephen's Island, New Zealand
1894

The true story of Tibbles the cat made a huge impact on the world by alerting humans to the dangers of introducing non-native plants and animals—in this case, house cats—to other parts of the world. It's a story we can all learn from, as today, tragically, the Stephens Island wren lives on only in museums—in the form of taxidermy specimens.

Tibbles was a curious cat from England who excitingly found herself on a small island off the coast of New Zealand in 1894. Little did anyone know what would result from such a seemingly harmless pet. This true story reminds us that introducing non-native animals to new environments can have unintended—oftentimes disastrous—consequences. But by learning from this little cat's big mistakes, we can make sure we don't repeat them.

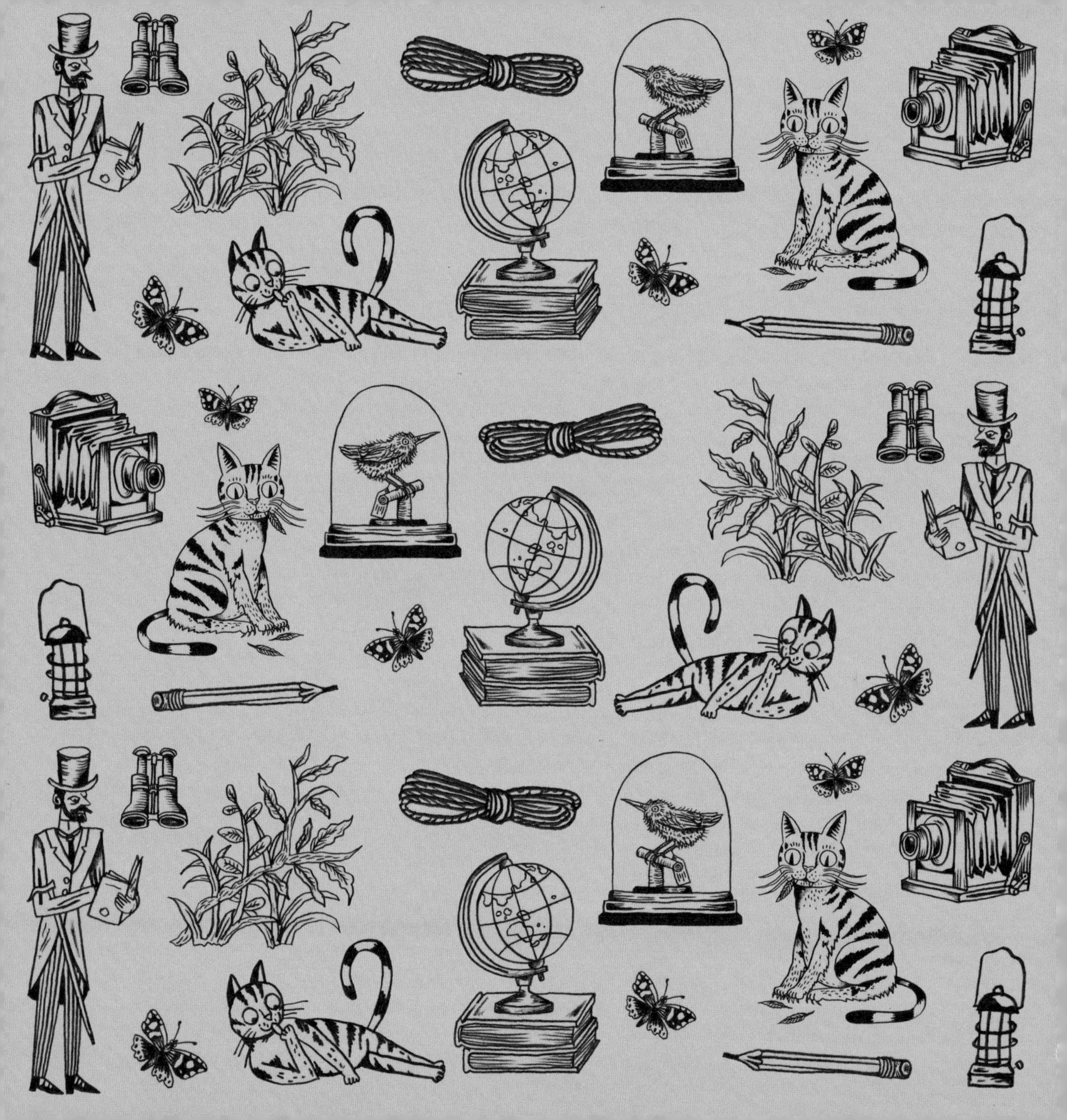